COUNTING BOOK OF
BUGS
Count from 1 to 13
by Cathy Cawood

*This book is dedicated to my brother Wayne,
who used to catch a lot of woodlice
and also to my student Airi,
a girl who likes bugs!*

Many thanks to the wonderful photographers at Pixabay.com
who supplied most of the images in this book.

The small cicada image on page 37 was created by Nicolas Raymond
an is licensed under the Creative Commons Attribution 3.0 Unported License.
To view a copy of this license, visit http://creativecommons.org/licenses/by/3.0/
or send a letter to Creative Commons, PO Box 1866, Mountain View, CA 94042, USA.
I removed the background and adjusted the color and contrast.

Published by Cathleen Cawood
www.kidsbooksandgames.weebly.com

1, 2, 3, 4, 5 little ladybugs

6, 7, 8, 9, 10 little ladybugs

11
12
13

little
ladybugs
crawling all day long!

1, 2, 3, 4, 5 little grasshoppers

6, 7, 8, 9, 10 little grasshoppers

11
12
13

little
grasshoppers
jumping all day long!

1, 2, 3, 4, 5 little butterflies

6, 7, 8, 9, 10 little butterflies

11
12
13

little
butterflies
flying all day long!

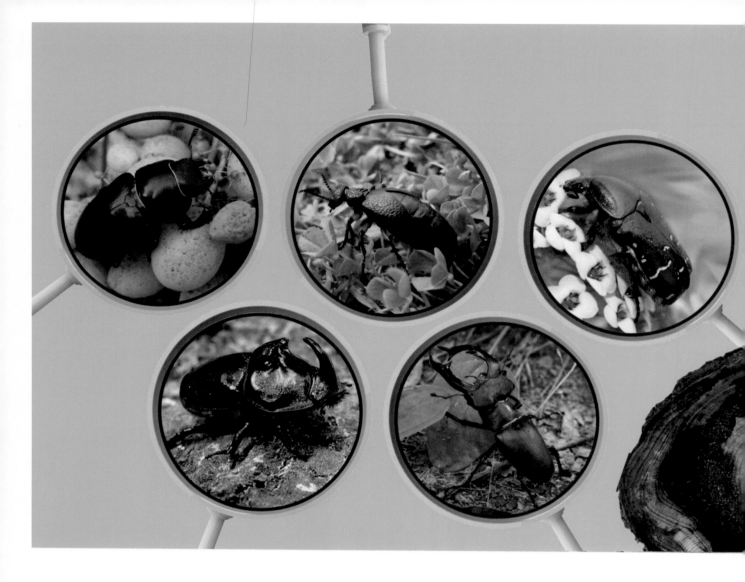

1, 2, 3, 4, 5 little beetles

6, 7, 8, 9, 10 little beetles

11
12
13

little
beetles
crawling all day long!

1, 2, 3, 4, 5 little dragonflies

6, 7, 8, 9, 10 little dragonflies

11
12
13
little
dragonflies
flying all day long!

1, 2, 3, 4, 5 little caterpillars

6, 7, 8, 9, 10 little caterpillars

11
12
13

little
caterpillars
eating all day long!

1, 2, 3, 4, 5 little honey bees

6, 7, 8, 9, 10 little honey bees

11
12
13

little
honey bees
working all day long!

1, 2, 3, 4, 5 little snails

6, 7, 8, 9, 10 little snails

11
12
13
little
snails
crawling all day long!

1, 2, 3, 4, 5 little cicadas

6, 7, 8, 9, 10 little cicadas

11
12
13

little
cicadas
singing all day long!

1, 2, 3, 4, 5 little ants

6, 7, 8, 9, 10 little ants

11
12
13

little

ants

working all day long!

Printed in Great Britain
by Amazon